10/13

GREEN-
COLLAR
CAREERS

TOURING, TREKKING, AND TRAVELING GREEN

CAREERS IN ECOTOURISM

By Diane Dakers

CRABTREE
Publishing Company
www.crabtreebooks.com

Crabtree Publishing Company

Author: Diane Dakers
Contributing author: Ruth Owen
Publishing plan research and development:
    Sean Charlebois, Reagan Miller
    Crabtree Publishing Company
Editors: Mark Sachner, Molly Aloian
Proofreader: Crystal Sikkens
Editorial director: Kathy Middleton
Photo research: Ruth Owen
Designer: Westgrapix/Tammy West
Production coordinator: Margaret Amy Salter
Prepress technician: Margaret Amy Salter
Print coordinator: Katherine Berti
Production: Kim Richardson
Curriculum adviser: Suzy Gazlay, M.A.

Written, developed, and produced by Water
Buffalo Books

Photographs and reproductions:
Marc Bartschat: page 53.
Corbis: Jon Hicks: page 10; James Morgan: page 34
(bottom); Matthieu Paley: page 49.
Ecoscene: Bjorn Svensson: page 17; Chinch Gryniewicz:
page 33 (top); Chinch Gryniewicz: page 35.
FLPA: Elliott Neep: page 6; Jean Hosking: page 7; Ingrid
Visser: page 19 (top); Pete Oxford: page 19 (bottom); Oliver
Gerhard: page 33 (bottom); Ariadne Van Zandbergen: page
40 (top); Ariadne Van Zandbergen: pages 40–41 (main); Suzi
Eszterhaus: pages 44–45; Norbert Wu: page 47; Norbert
Eisele-Hein: page 54; page 57.
Shutterstock: cover; page 1; pages 4–5; page 8; page 9; page
11; page 12; page 13; page 14; page 15; page 16; page 18;
pages 20–21; pages 22–23; pages 24–25; page 26; pages
28–29; pages 30–31; page 34 (top); page 36; page 37; page 38;
page 39; page 42; page 43; page 46; page 48; page 50; page
51; page 52; page 56; page 58.
John Voci: page 55.
Wikipedia Creative Commons (public domain): page 27.

Library and Archives Canada Cataloguing in Publication

Dakers, Diane
    Touring, trekking, and traveling green : careers in ecotourism /
Diane Dakers.

(Green-collar careers)
Includes index.
Issued also in electronic format.
ISBN 978-0-7787-4859-5 (bound).--ISBN 978-0-7787-4870-0 (pbk.)

    1. Ecotourism--Vocational guidance--Juvenile literature.
2. Travel--Environmental aspects--Juvenile literature. I. Title.
II. Series: Green-collar careers

G156.5.E26D35 2011   j338.4'791   C2011-902862-X

Library of Congress Cataloging-in-Publication Data

Dakers, Diane.
  Touring, trekking, and traveling green : careers in ecotourism / Diane
Dakers.
      p. cm. -- (Green collar careers.)
  Includes index.
  ISBN 978-0-7787-4859-5 (reinforced library binding : alk. paper) --
ISBN 978-0-7787-4870-0 (pbk. : alk. paper) -- ISBN 978-1-4271-9723-8
(electronic pdf)
1. Ecotourism--Vocational guidance. 2. Green movement--Vocational
guidance. 3. Green technology--Vocational guidance. I. Title. II. Series.

  G156.5.E26D34 2012
  320.5'8--dc23

                                                          2011015542

Crabtree Publishing Company
www.crabtreebooks.com   1-800-387-7650

Printed in China/082011/TM20110511

Published in Canada
Crabtree Publishing
616 Welland Ave.
St. Catharines, Ontario
L2M 5V6

Published in the United States
Crabtree Publishing
PMB 59051
350 Fifth Avenue, 59th Floor
New York, New York 10118

Published in the United Kingdom
Crabtree Publishing
Maritime House
Basin Road North, Hove
BN41 1WR

Published in Australia
Crabtree Publishing
3 Charles Street
Coburg North
VIC 305

CONTENTS

TAKE ONLY PHOTOS, LEAVE ONLY FOOTPRINTS

Travel Agent

A giraffe looks out over the Nile River in Africa. The ecotourism business is committed to helping travelers explore beautiful places like this. It is also committed to helping these places survive!

Visiting a beautiful, faraway country that is very different from your own is a thrilling experience. You have the opportunity to see breathtaking landscapes, plants, and animals that you don't see at home. You might even have the chance to learn how people in another part of the world live.

Finding a Match for a Green Lifestyle

If traveling and exploration are in your blood, you might have wondered what it would be like to work in tourism. This industry helps more than 900 million people worldwide plan and enjoy tours and vacations each year. You may also want to live an eco-friendly life, and you care about issues such as saving energy and reducing pollution.

Writer

Tourism is big business! Billions of dollars are spent each year on vacations. If tourism were a country, it would have an economy second only to that of the United States. Tourism also provides jobs for millions of people—from tour guides working in the field, to office workers who make bookings. This means the tourism industry has the power to be a huge force for good!

Eco-Lodge Worker

Tour Guide

Park Ranger

MARINE WILDLIFE TOUR GUIDE AND BOAT SKIPPER

I run my own business giving marine wildlife-watching tours by boat. We are based in Cornwall in the Southwest of England.

I started wildlife guiding when I was 17, working as a crew member and guide on tourist boats. Today, I take groups of 12 people out on an R.I.B. (rigid inflatable boat) to see whales, dolphins, seals, basking sharks, and many different species of seabirds. My company also offers safari-style walking tours that teach visitors about Cornwall's wildlife, plants, geology, folklore, and mining history. Elemental Tours operates a "visitor payback" scheme, which means that part of the fees for our tours goes to wildlife and conservation charities.

We were founding members of the WiSe scheme, which is an accreditation scheme that ensures marine wildlife-watching boats operate in a way that is not harmful or disruptive for the animals. We are also ambassadors for CoaST (Cornwall Sustainable Tourism project). This is a network of businesses working to help tourism create social, economic, and environmental benefits for all.

You can achieve so much more in this field than just doing a job. I highly recommend working in this industry as a career.

Rory Goodall
Boat skipper and Company Director
Elemental Tours
Penzance, Cornwall, England

DEPAR

ED NEW TIME
TO
PORTLAND
PORTLAND
BANGKOK
JAKARTA
BANGALORE
SHENYANG
SHENYANG
SHENYANG
SHENYANG
SHENYANG
SHENYANG
TAIPEI

If so, how can you match your green lifestyle with a career that involves traveling thousands of miles and visiting places that could be damaged by the arrival of busloads of outsiders?

Maybe you're not an adventurer, but you try to be eco-friendly. Protecting wild habitats and endangered plants and animals is important to you. You might also want to help people in other parts of the world who live in poverty and are struggling to survive.

The Right Career for You?

If either travel or helping the planet sounds like your kind of life, a career in ecotourism could be for you. Ecotourism is a fast-growing area of the travel industry.

Tourists take a tiger safari in India. Bengal tigers are critically endangered, and funds from "tiger watching" help conservation projects protect the animals and manage protected national parks. The tourists are carried by Asian elephants. The tigers accept the elephants coming close to them because the elephants are a natural part of the tigers' habitat. The elephants are also less environmentally damaging than jeeps or other gas-powered safari vehicles.

You could find yourself leading an educational hike through a protected rain forest. Closer to home, you might work for an organization that helps people in Africa or Asia earn money by taking care of foreign travelers and showing them the history or natural wonders of their local area.

So what exactly is ecotourism?

Ecotourism—Making Tourism Count

The International Ecotourism Society (TIES) defines ecotourism as follows: "Responsible travel to natural areas that conserves the environment and improves the well-being of local people."

A spotter looks out for wildlife from the front of a safari jeep in Botswana, Africa. Spotters have a lot of experience at finding wild animals. They are also very knowledgeable about wildlife and the local habitat and can answer visitors' questions. A safari company might be based in London or New York, but the company will employ local African people as spotters and guides for their safaris.

THE PRINCIPLES OF ECOTOURISM

The International Ecotourism Society (TIES) lists the key features of ecotourism as follows:

• Minimize impact.
Travelers should not leave behind garbage or pollute wild habitats.

• Build environmental and cultural awareness and respect.
Travelers learn about the animals and plants in a wild habitat. They learn about indigenous people and their way of life but do not treat them as a sideshow!

• Provide positive experiences for both visitors and hosts.
Travelers come to understand a different way of life, while their hosts may learn more about the wildlife or habitat around them by working as rangers.

• Provide direct financial benefits for conservation.
Part of the money paid by travelers for their vacation is used for projects that protect wild habitats and endangered animals.

• Provide financial benefits and empowerment for local people.
Ecotourism companies aim to employ as many local people as possible. Jobs could involve building projects and providing services to visitors as tour guides or hotel workers.

• Raise sensitivity to host countries' political, environmental, and social climate.
Travelers learn about the problems faced by communities in developing countries if, for example, their country has been at war or they have suffered floods or droughts.

Ecotourism is all about the conservation, or protection, of the natural world. It means traveling in a way that is sustainable. This means the traveler does not damage a place for the future. Ecotourism also means bringing together foreign travelers and indigenous, or local, people in a way that is respectful to those people. Ecotourism allows outsiders to learn about another culture while helping local people keep their culture alive by earning money from the visits.

Ecotourism trips might be day trips, two-week vacations, or adventure tours that last for weeks or months. Travelers might want to relax on a beach, scuba dive, or climb mountains. They might want to visit ancient buildings or carry out hands-on work with endangered animals. Ecotourism has something for everyone!

Ecotourism is not just about looking and watching. It's also all about doing! If you love outdoor pursuits or extreme sports, you might find a career working for an adventure company that offers extreme outdoor experiences in stunning locations around the world.

THE IMPORTANCE OF TOURIST DOLLARS

- In four out of five countries worldwide, tourism is one of the top five ways that the country earns export income (money from other countries).

- Tourism is the main export for one-third of the world's poorest countries.

- In 2006, $735 billion was spent on tourism. Of this amount, $221 billion went to developing countries in poorer parts of the world.

From a Dark Past to a Bright Future

In the villages of Albreda and Juffureh (also spelled *Jufureh* and *Juffure*) in Gambia, Africa, people are proud to keep alive the story of how their ancestors were forced to become slaves. The famous book *Roots*, by Alex Haley, told the story of Kunta Kinte, a young man from the village of Juffureh who was forced to become a slave. Many tourists from North America and Europe who had read the book visited the villages. The local people benefited very little from these visits, however. No fees were paid to the villagers, and they had no say about the tourists coming to their homes.

Textiles for sale in a Malaysian market (top) and jewelry for sale in India (bottom). Selling locally made goods to tourists can be an important source of income for many people worldwide.

A traditionally dressed woman from an Akha hill tribe sells locally made crafts in a village in Thailand. Some tour companies work with the Akha people to offer tours that allow visitors to sit in on lessons at an Akha school, visit farms, and learn how to cook traditional hill tribe food in the villagers' homes.

THE INVENTION OF ECOTOURISM

The term "ecotourism" and its definition were coined in 1983 by a Mexican environmentalist named Hector Ceballos-Lascurain. Hector was an architect who specialized in designing eco-friendly buildings. Hector has combined his skills for designing green places with his love of conservation to help create tourist destinations that are eco-friendly and sustainable. Organizations around the world have used his expert help when developing ecotourism projects.

A charity in the United Kingdom called the Travel Foundation began working with the villagers. Its goal was to help the villagers benefit from their history. Now, tours visit the villages, and money from each tour goes to a village fund. Tourist dollars have helped pay for a children's center. There, children can be educated, play, and learn traditional crafts. Local people have been trained to be tour guides, and they earn a monthly salary. Traditional crafts have been revived. These include the making of tie-dyed fabrics that are unique to the area. These crafts are sold to the tourists.

Each year, about 10,000 tourists go on this tour. Tourism helps keep the story of this community alive, and it is doing so in a way that will benefit the people into the future.

An antislavery statue faces the Gambia River and dock in Juffureh, Gambia. Tourist boats stop here so that visitors can tour the villages of Juffureh and Albreda and learn more about the history of this region.

Different Labels, Same Goals

When you are planning a vacation or looking at career options for the future, you might come across the terms "responsible travel" and "sustainable tourism." There is a lot of crossover between ecotourism and responsible travel. They both aim to achieve many of the same things. Sustainable tourism is a tourism experience that does not damage a destination or the lives of the people who live there. It is also about creating tourism opportunities that will go on helping local people into the future.

The different labels can be confusing! Just remember that in the past tourism has caused a lot of damage to Earth. The people who plan to work in tourism in the future must be committed to making tourism a positive thing for people and the planet!

A street vendor sells freshly made Thai food to tourists in a market. Around 80 percent of the money from traditional all-inclusive package vacations goes to big-name hotel chains, airlines, and large international companies. Ecotour operators encourage travelers to spend their money on accommodations, food, and activities offered by local people.

WHAT IS CLIMATE CHANGE?

Climate change is the gradual increase of Earth's temperature. Today, most scientists agree that this increase is caused by humans burning fossil fuels, such as oil and coal. Burning fossil fuels releases harmful gases, such as carbon dioxide (CO_2), methane, and nitrous oxide, into the atmosphere. These gases have become known as "greenhouse gases." This is because they trap heat from the Sun on Earth, just as the glass of a greenhouse traps heat.

Our planet needs heat and light from the Sun in order for life to exist on Earth. Too much heat is a bad thing, however. Parts of the world may become too dry for food to grow. Weather may become more extreme, resulting in hurricanes, heat waves, and torrential rain. Glaciers and the giant ice caps at the north and south poles will melt. This will cause ocean levels to rise. Some scientists predict that if all the ice in the planet's glaciers melted, ocean levels would rise by over 200 feet (60 meters). Low-lying cities, such as New York and London, would disappear under water!

How Has Tourism Damaged Our Planet?

One of the challenges our planet is facing is climate change-our planet is slowly getting warmer. This is known as global warming. Sadly, tourism has played a part in the warming of our planet.

Global warming is caused by the release of greenhouse gases into the atmosphere. Greenhouse gases include carbon dioxide (CO_2), methane, and nitrous oxide. It has been estimated that global tourism is responsible for nearly five percent of the world's CO_2 emissions. Of the emissions created by tourism, over 75 percent come from travel. Much of this figure comes from air travel. There are plans that travelers can now use to help reduce the effects of CO_2 emissions when they fly. We will look at these plans, called carbon offsetting, in chapter two.

When touring in hot places, tour buses often leave their engines running for long periods of time, even when they are parked. Tourists can then return to an air-conditioned bus after their sightseeing excursion. Unfortunately, this practice also increases CO_2 emissions into the atmosphere.

It's not just traveling to a destination that causes damage. Many popular holiday destinations are in hot, dry places. Fresh water in these areas can be scarce. Tourism means that hotels fill up swimming pools. Meanwhile, thousands of tourists flush toilets and take showers. Golfing holidays are very popular. To keep the grass lush and green at a golf course in a tropical country such as Thailand can use as much water in one year as 60,000 local people would have used!

Building hotels and resorts often requires clearing forests and spoiling untouched coastlines. Hotels use large amounts of energy to run air-conditioning systems and heat swimming pools. Even tourists trekking in mountains may leave behind garbage and unwanted equipment.

This lush, green, 18-hole golf course in Thailand can soak up over two million quarts (1.9 million liters) of water a day!

COULD YOU BE AN ECOTOURIST?

An ecotourist can have a wide variety of interests. Do any of these characteristics sound like you? If so, then you might make a great ecotourist, or even someone who works in the field!

- You switch off lights and walk or cycle instead of riding in the car because you want to save energy.

- You save water whenever possible.

- You reuse things and recycle.

- You try to eat foods that are organic and have been grown or produced by companies local to you.

- You support organizations that are caring for wild places or endangered animals.

- You watch news items about people in other countries who are in trouble and want to know what you can do to help.

- You want to see as many amazing places in the world as possible!

- You are interested in seeing the real life of a place, not just the main tourist attractions.

- You are eager to learn other languages.

- You're happy when the money you spend helps other individuals and supports small businesses instead of giant, faceless companies.

Picnickers and other visitors have left behind soda cans, bottles, food wrappings, and other trash in a forest.

The World Needs Ecotourism

The ongoing environmental damage to our planet means that we've had to rethink tourism. This means traveling in ways that reduce CO_2 emissions, cut down on pollution, and protect natural habitats. Ecotourism companies help their customers vacation in a way that does not damage wild places. They also use some of the money they make to support conservation projects.

One example of ecotourism at its best may be found at the Chumbe Island Coral Park. This is a tiny coral island surrounded by coral reefs just off the coast of Zanzibar, in Tanzania, Africa. Tourists can stay on the island and spend their days snorkeling. There, they see an amazing display of coral and marine life.

Some of that wildlife, such as the critically endangered hawksbill turtle, opens their eyes to both the beauty and the fragility of this amazing habitat. The tourists not only learn about the ecology of the island and surrounding waters. They also stay in eco-friendly, tent-like bungalows. These bungalows use solar power, and rainwater is collected for use in the bathrooms.

The money from tourism is used to protect and care for the coral reef. Local people work as guides and rangers, taking visitors on educational tours and protecting this special habitat.

A scuba diver photographs a critically endangered hawksbill turtle as it swims over a coral reef.

TRAVELING THE ECOTOURISM WAY

Here are just some of the things that travelers can do to make their vacations kinder to people and the environment:

- Do a lot of research in advance so you can use tour companies and stay in places that support ecotourism.

- Ask your hotel what THEY are doing to protect the environment.

- Ask the workers in your hotel about their jobs. Are the people treated well by the hotel owners?

- Cut down on those trips to McDonald's! Eat in small restaurants owned by local people.

- Walk or cycle when touring around or use public transportation such as buses.

- Learn some of the country's language so that you can speak to local people.

Continued on page 17...

Ecotourism makes a profit for companies big and small, but it uses some of that profit to help nature and people alike. Ecotourism provides jobs for millions of people worldwide. Ecotourism also gives people who care about the planet the ability to enjoy wonderful travel experiences while helping protect the planet and improve the lives of people who are less fortunate.

Beware! When Green Is Not All It Seems

As demand for ecotourism grows, some businesses are hoping to benefit without putting in the work! Some travel agents, resorts, and other tourism businesses that advertise themselves as "eco" or "green" have really only made the smallest of changes to how they do business.

Right and opposite page: Over 85 percent of the world's coral reefs are damaged. They are damaged by sewage that is spilled into the ocean from nearby towns and resorts. They are also damaged by the anchors of cruise ships. Unthinking tourists tear off pieces, and local people sometimes harvest coral to sell to tourists.

This practice is known as "greenwashing." It comes from the term "whitewashing," which means deliberately covering something up.

Some hotels might install showers that use less water. Others might offer some organic foods on their menu. Both of these actions are great for the environment, but they don't add up to ecotourism! The hotel is simply using "green" as a way to catch the eye of eco-friendly tourists without doing as much as it could to help the planet. Travelers need to do their research, ask a lot of questions, and dig deep to find out which companies are truly eco-friendly and which are just greenwashing!

TRAVELING THE ECOTOURISM WAY

...continued from page 16

• Always ask if you can photograph someone, and ask permission before going into a sacred place or onto someone's land.

• Don't haggle over prices too much! Pay a fair price to people selling locally made items.

• Never buy coral, seashells, or craft items made from endangered animals—for example, items made from ivory. An elephant had to die for that souvenir to be made!

• Stick to paths and marked trails in wild habitats and don't disturb or frighten wild animals.

• Never drop litter, and try to bring any unwanted items, such as empty shampoo bottles, home with you. This way, your trash does not become someone else's problem.

Could Ecotourism Be Your Future?

There is a famous saying: Take only photos, leave only footprints. It means that travelers should not take from the environment or leave any damaging mark on it. It's a good thought for someone interested in ecotourism to keep in mind. Ecotourism can leave some marks on the world, though—positive ones! It can ensure that a wild place remains exactly as it is for the future. It can change the lives of a community of people forever.

There are many different careers available in ecotourism. A few years from now you could be working as a travel agent or tour guide. You might be researching and writing about ecotourism for newspapers and magazines. Perhaps leading a group of scuba divers around a coral reef or being the onboard expert on a whale-watching boat is for you. You might even be managing an eco-hotel, or working as a yoga teacher at an eco-friendly camp deep in a forest.

By the year 2020 it is estimated that 1.56 billion people each year will be traveling the world as tourists. Maybe YOU could be one of the workers helping those people be eco-travelers!

PLEASE TAKE NOTHING BUT PICTURES LEAVE NOTHING BUT FOOTPRINTS

GREEN VACATIONS—A WORLD OF OPPORTUNITY!

Don't get green with envy, but here are just two of the fantastic vacations available through travel companies that offer their customers eco-friendly adventures.

• **Cruise around the Arctic island of Spitsbergen, Norway.**

Living on a small cruise ship, travelers on this expedition will sail between snow-covered mountains and vast areas of ice. They will see walruses, Arctic foxes, whales, and polar bears. The tourism company gives funds to many Arctic conservation projects.

Just feet from this polar bear on an ice floe, passengers on an ecotourism Arctic cruise ship get to see the world's largest land predator on its own "turf"!

Travelers know that part of their fee is going toward a good cause. For example, the company buys tracking collars for polar bears. These collars send signals to satellites and back to scientists who follow the bears. This helps scientists collect valuable information on where the bears go to hunt and how they are being affected by climate change.

• **Explore the Amazon Rain Forest by canoe.**

On this tour, small groups of travelers use eco-friendly canoes to explore the South American country of Ecuador. Local guides teach the travelers about the culture and history of the people in the area and the plants and animals. Visitors stay in small hotels owned by local people and spend two nights staying with Amazon Quichua people in their homes. This gives visitors a chance to learn about the

Using only people power, these tourists are traveling through the Amazon Rain Forest in Ecuador in dugout canoes.

lifestyle and customs of the Quichua people. Funds from these tours have been used for many projects that improve the lives of the Quichua, including the building of a schoolhouse.

HOW IT ALL BEGINS

Before setting off on a vacation, most travelers research and plan their trips. Some might be inspired to visit a particular country by reading a magazine article. Others may spend time looking at Web sites to get ideas.

A Creative Career in Green Travel

Once they have an idea of where they would like to go, travelers might buy a guidebook. This is a great way to begin planning excursions and learn more about the area they are visiting. Guidebooks are written by travel writers.

As a travel writer, you will get to try out and review the activities that tour operators offer. You might be kayaking one week and climbing mountains the next!

These people have the dream job of traveling the world, researching the places they visit, and then reporting back on the best, and sometimes worst, places to take a vacation!

With the popularity of ecotourism rising, a special breed of writers will be more and more in demand. These are writers who care about green issues and are exploring ways to travel that support the principles of ecotourism.

Most travel writers are freelance. This means they are self-employed and work for a lot of different companies on a job-by-job basis. A writer may be contacted by a magazine or travel guide publisher and be asked to write an article or book.

Travel writers review hotels, restaurants, bars, and other places that offer travelers food, drink, and lodging. Green travel writers will be on the lookout for locally sourced food. They will also write about water- and energy-saving initiatives, as well as the ways in which businesses create employment for local people.

Alternatively, a writer may have his or her own idea, write an article, and then try to sell it to a magazine. A career as a freelance green travel writer could be for you if you are an engaging and creative writer and don't want to be tied down to one job. It also helps if you would like to be able to travel while you are working. All this goes for travel Web sites, too!

Publishers that produce green travel guides also employ editors. These are the people who make sure the text reads well and is grammatically and factually correct. Publishers also need graphic designers, whose job it is to make the pages of a magazine or book look beautiful.

Without photographers, we wouldn't know what to expect from the places we choose for trips and vacations. Like writers, travel photographers are normally freelance. They visit exotic locations and take photographs of people and places. They then sell the photographs to magazines, newspapers, and book publishers.

Does the thought of your work appearing online appeal to you? If so, remember that most of these jobs can be applied to the Internet and travel Web sites, too!

Capturing the perfect shot can mean hours of patience in less than ideal conditions! However, working as a travel photographer will allow you to experience new places, people, and cultures.

"The foreign travel is a huge plus point! I also love hearing back from my clients when they've had a great time away on a holiday I've organized for them. Positive feedback gives me a real buzz."

Hannah Savege,
Africa Travel Coordinator,
Tribes Travel,
Suffolk, UK

It's All Under Control!

When you are on vacation with your family, are you the one who wants to be sure that not a second of the trip is wasted? Are you the one who checks out the guidebook and pores over leaflets promoting places to go? Perhaps, when your friends are bored during the school holidays, you are the one who plans exciting days out for everyone. If so, maybe your future career in ecotourism could be as a travel agent.

Just like a traditional travel agent, an ecotourism travel agent will help his or her customers plan their vacations. You will be working for a company that plans and sells a variety of different trips to travelers.

The agent puts together an itinerary of the trip for the customer. An itinerary is a day-by-day plan of where travelers will go, how they will get there, where they will stay, and what they will see and do. Agents must have a good knowledge of which hotels and resorts are eco-friendly. They will also be able to plan activities for the customer that will benefit local communities or help conservation projects.

As an ecotourism travel agent, you might be planning a trip for a senior couple looking to cycle across a country in Asia. You might book an adventure holiday for 20 teens who want to camp, kayak, and get hands-on with a conservation project miles from civilization!

Your clients need to fly from Canada to South Africa. They want to experience camping. They want to see wild animals in their natural habitat. Their hobby is birdwatching. As a travel agent, it's your job to create a trip that encompasses all their requests.

CAREER PROFILE

MAKING DREAM VACATIONS COME TRUE: ECO-TRAVEL AGENT

I create custom-made vacations to Africa using accommodations and suppliers who have good eco-credentials whenever possible. I look after clients from the moment they inquire all the way through the planning and booking process, and until they get back home. I book all flights, accommodations, and excursions. I also look after all the admin work for each booking and deal with any issues that crop up along the way.

This job isn't about the hard sell; it's about building up relationships with people over time, sometimes even months, until you find them exactly what they're looking for. I juggle a lot of clients at once, so I have to be very organized.

I went to University to study Third World Development. After I graduated, I did some sales work and then I took myself off traveling to Africa. I worked in Kenya building a school for five weeks and then traveled overland from Nairobi to Cape Town, South Africa. When I came back, I saw this job advertised. I had the travel experience and some sales experience, so I applied—and the rest is history!

The best part is that I get at least one educational trip to Africa each year. So far I've been sent to Tanzania, Zanzibar, and Botswana.

Hannah Savege
Africa Travel Coordinator
Tribes Travel
Suffolk, UK

TRAVEL GUIDES YOU CAN WATCH

Wildside (UK) Productions is a London-based company that produces films and TV shows. Wildside focuses on making informative, educational films about the environment, conservation issues, and sustainability. The company also works in ecotourism. Green Travel Guides TV is an online service that features a series of Internet television shows produced by Wildside. The shows are all about incredible vacation destinations, such as Antarctica or the Costa Rican rain forest. The online TV shows give eco-friendly tourists inspiration for places to visit and help them make the greenest choices possible. Not only does the creative team at Wildside work in the exciting world of film making. They also get to travel the world and help protect the planet!

Your job will be to make sure that your customers have the best time possible and do the most to help the planet and the people they meet along the way.

The Right Person for the Job

A travel agent must be good with people. You will deal with customers face to face, by telephone, and by email. If things go wrong, you will be the one to help your customers when they are thousands of miles from home. You must be organized and good with details. After all, it doesn't do the customers or your business any good if they are waiting for a train at 11:00 A.M. and it left the station at 9:00! You may also need to learn foreign languages so you can phone hotels or tour operators in other countries.

As a travel agent, you help your clients plan every detail of their trip. If something goes wrong during their vacation, you need to be a good problem solver to get the trip back on track fast!

There's a lot to juggle, but there are a lot of terrific advantages as well. One big bonus is that as a travel agent, you will receive good discounts on your own travel to faraway places. You will also have fantastic insider knowledge of all the best places to go!

Getting the Message Out There

Another key role in promoting and selling eco-vacations is marketing. This career involves a wide variety of activities and skills. These include advertising, selling, understanding what customers want, and developing new things to offer customers. It may also include public relations, which is making sure the outside world knows all the good things about your company! One day, you might be talking to travelers to find out what they thought about your company's latest tours.

CARBON OFFSETTING— MAKING AIR TRAVEL GREENER

One of the biggest problems with any type of tourism is the amount of greenhouse gases released by the burning of aviation fuel. Even if your vacation destination is very green, your flight, which could cover thousands of miles, won't be! The way that many eco-friendly travelers deal with this is by a system called carbon offsetting.

When air travelers book a flight or a vacation, they can calculate the amount of carbon dioxide (CO_2) that will be released by their journey. The traveler then makes a payment that goes to a project that will offset, or reduce, that amount of CO_2 being released. For example, a flight from London to Bangkok will create 1,874 pounds (850 kilograms) of CO_2. The payment the traveler makes will go toward an environmentally friendly energy project, such as a wind farm, that will prevent 1,874 pounds of CO_2 from being released into the atmosphere.

Every legitimate carbon offset program contains a full set of details and statistics about the way the program works and how the money is used.

A bird's-eye view of Terminal 5 at London's Heathrow Airport. Heathrow is one of the world's busiest airports. In 2009, 460,000 flights took off or landed at the airport!

GOING GREEN IN THE CONCRETE JUNGLE

Ecotourism doesn't have to just be about jungles and wild places! What about travelers who crave the buzz of a big city? When you think of a city such as New York or London, you may not think "green," but a city-based vacation can be very eco-friendly. Cities such as New York have mass transit systems to get you wherever you need to go. Tourists can choose an eco-friendly hotel and eat at the many organic or small family-owned restaurants that are available.

Visitors to New York can take a guided cycle tour through Central Park. They can also take themed walking tours that offer everything from the history of New York's architecture to sites in Central Park that have been featured in movies! A visitor to New York may even want to take in a baseball game at the New York Mets' eco-friendly Citi Field. The stadium was built using 95 percent recycled steel, and its green initiatives include plumbing systems that will save around four million gallons (15 million liters) of water each year!

What type of vacation is your company selling? Are they targeting seniors, honeymoon couples, families, or adventurers? Understanding who your potential customer will be is an important part of developing a successful marketing campaign.

The next day, you might be developing an online campaign to raise awareness for a conservation project your company is supporting as part of one of its vacations. There are millions of green travelers out there, and your job will be to make sure they choose your company's vacations.

Today, a lot of marketing is done online. You could be organizing an email campaign to the people on your company's database. You could be blogging about the latest tour your company is offering to India.

You might also be setting up a Facebook campaign to publicize the work your company is doing with endangered wildlife in Africa.

A Worldwide Team

Ecotourism companies do all they can to employ local people in the countries where their vacations are set. But behind-the-scenes teams who promote and sell the vacations are often in places such as North America or Europe. This offers you a great opportunity to work within this industry and stay close to family and friends.

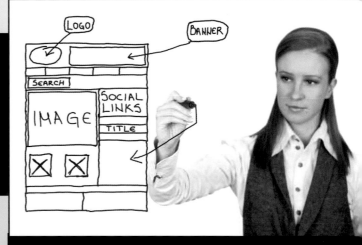

Could your future role in ecotourism involve designing a Web site that will inspire people to travel the eco way?

DREAM VACATIONS, DREAM JOBS

O ne very important feature of any vacation is the place where you stay. You might be staying on a campsite, in a small guesthouse, or in a vast hotel that houses hundreds of people.

A large hotel development under construction. Sewage from hotels can end up in the ocean. There, this waste can damage coral reefs and harm the local marine life.

The building of tourist accommodations has been responsible for damaging many wild habitats. Coniferous (evergreen and cone-bearing) forests are cleared to make space for ski resorts. Coastal wetlands, places that are home to many species of aquatic plants and animals, are often used as land on which to build beach resorts. The sandy beaches that attract tourists are allowed to stay.

Meanwhile, the wetlands become a construction site for hotels, restaurants, employee accommodations, parking, and roads in and out of the resorts.

Helping Nature Help Us

Mangrove swamps are often found along the coastlines of tropical countries. Large mangrove plants grow in shallow waters. Their many tangled roots protect the coast by forming a natural barrier between the sea and land. The swamps are also home to many animals and plants. In some places, mangrove swamps have been cleared to build resorts and marinas, places where yachts and other boats can be moored. When the 2004 Indian Ocean tsunami hit the coastlines of Indonesia, the results were devastating. Areas that still had protective mangrove swamps suffered far less damage, though.

Coastal wetlands (above) and mangrove swamps (below) are home to many different species of mammals, birds, fish, amphibians, insects, and plants. These important habitats are often the victim of coastal tourism developments.

OWNING AND MANAGING A RAIN FOREST ECOLODGE

The inspiration behind our business was traveling in Central America and a love of nature. My wife and I wanted to build a remote adventure lodge with as little impact on the Earth as possible.

As the owner and general manager, I work in all aspects of the business including operations (day-to-day running of the hotel), finance, and marketing.

I have a master's degree in urban planning and did undergraduate work in political science-sociology. My career prior to this was in urban revitalization and community development work. I was also involved in real estate development. I was a big traveler and nature lover and had spent a lot of time traveling around Costa Rica. My wife, Donna, had a background in environmental planning, park planning, and conservation. Donna also loved the outdoor life. Together our skills made this vision come together.

There is never an average day on the job. Managing a team of over 20 employees and making sure the guest experience is fantastic takes a great deal of behind-the-scenes work.

We have had many, many memorable events and adventures, but I think we'll always remember what it was like to develop the lodge. To build the lodge, we had to bring all the materials by boat. Sometimes it seemed that there were obstacles every day, but eventually the dream was completed and the lodge was built.

If you want to start an ecotourism business, follow your dreams and find out exactly what area you want to concentrate on. Talk to as many people as possible in the field and do your research!

Michael Butler
Owner and Operator
Playa Nicuesa Rainforest Lodge,
Costa Rica

Staying in Tune with Nature

One important area of ecotourism is the building of visitor accommodations that are in harmony with nature. This type of accommodation is known as an ecolodge. An ecolodge can be a hotel. It can also be a place with a communal building for eating and socializing, with individual bungalows, cabins, huts, or even tents where the guests sleep.

Ecolodges are built using local labor. They are also created in the architectural style of the region, often using designs developed by local craftspeople. Many ecolodges are built in forests. The buildings are positioned in natural clearings so no trees or other plants have to be cut down. The construction materials are sourced locally, and many are recycled.

This Costa Rican ecolodge is in the Juan Castro Blanco National Park.

Not only do the lodges offer a place to live and eat, but they may also offer their guests educational opportunities. These may include lectures, tours, or hikes that teach visitors about the plants and animals in the area. Visitors can also learn about the history and culture of the local people. Ecolodges even offer activities including kayaking, horseback riding, and fishing.

Most of the people who work in an ecolodge—the manager, chefs, food servers, and maintenance and housekeeping staff—will be people employed from nearby villages. This brings an important source of income into an area where jobs may be scarce.

Local craftsmen are using palm leaves to thatch the roof of a vacation cottage. The cottage is part of an eco-friendly resort in India called Our Native Village.

Working in an Ecolodge

Providing local employment is an important principle of ecotourism. Some jobs do, however, become available for people from outside the local community.

One way to get your career started could be to volunteer. Ecolodges sometimes have unpaid, voluntary positions available for English speakers. You might help with general duties, such as working in reception. You may be on call as a translator to help English-speaking visitors. You may even go on nature hikes with a local guide. If you are familiar with the local language, you could help translate between the tourists and the guide.

Voluntary positions often involve working on conservation projects. These might include planting trees or acting as an assistant to a scientist who is studying or doing a count of a particular species of bird or insect in the region. You might even help teach local children.

Ecolodges sometimes offer relaxation therapies, such as yoga, meditation, and massages. Perhaps you could combine travel with a career as a therapist or instructor at an ecolodge.

Staying in an ecolodge does not mean that travelers have to sacrifice luxury. This beautiful bedroom is part of an ecolodge in the Amazon Rain Forest in Ecuador.

ECO-LIVING IN AN ECOLODGE

Here are just some of the green measures taken by ecolodge owners Michael and Donna Butler in the building and running of their Costa Rican rain forest lodge:

- Visitors travel to the lodge by boat.

- The lodge was built with trees that fell naturally in the forest. Oxen pulled the trees from the forest.

- The lodge's roof tiles are made from recycled plastic, including plastic from the bags used by local banana growers.

- The buildings are positioned so they catch natural breezes from the beach and the mountains to cut down on the use of fans or air conditioning.

- Energy is produced using solar panels and recycled vegetable oil.

- Food is grown in the lodge gardens and purchased from local farmers.

- Food waste is composted and used as fertilizer for the crops in the garden.

- Eco-friendly cleaning products are used at all times.

- Gray water, which is waste water from bathing or doing dishes, is recycled for flushing toilets and other uses.

- Visitors use natural insect repellents made from onions, garlic, and chili peppers.

This is a natural swimming pool at the Our Native Village holiday resort in India. Instead of using chemicals to keep the water clean, the water is kept clean by aquatic plants.

COULD YOU START YOUR OWN ECOTOUR BUSINESS?

Do you love traveling? Are you a good organizer? If so, you have two of the basic requirements for running your own adventure tours business! Many colleges and universities offer courses in starting a travel business, and the Internet makes it possible for small businesses to promote their services without spending a vast amount of money.

In 1990, Bruce Poon Tip had just returned from a backpacking trip around Asia. Bruce wanted to help other people experience the adventure he had enjoyed, but he also wanted it to be done in a sustainable way. Bruce used his own credit cards to get the funds he needed to start up his adventure tours business. He called it Gap Adventures. Now Bruce's company offers eco-friendly vacations on every continent of the planet. Gap Adventures employs over 850 people worldwide in a wide variety of jobs from sales people in its offices, to tour guides out in the field.

It might sound like an impossible dream, but running your own adventure tours business could be your future destiny!

You might also help build a new school funded by the ecolodge for the local village. Volunteering will help teach you valuable lessons about how ecolodges operate. You will also increase your exposure to other languages and help local people improve their English.

Follow Me!
Life as a Tour Guide

Climbing a mountain, hiking through a jungle and meeting a local tribe, seeing a tiger emerge from a forest: These are all experiences that will make a traveler's dreams come true. It can be dangerous, however, for tourists to explore wild places without expert guidance. Unguided, they may also not get to see the things they wanted to see. They might not learn all there is to know about an area. This is where tour guides come in.

Making new friends of all ages could be just one of the benefits of working as a volunteer at an ecolodge. Getting research experience working on a conservation project will also look great on your resume as you develop your ecotourism career.

Working as a tour guide may mean leading a hike in the Australian desert or canoeing along a South American river. It might involve climbing onto a horse for trekking or getting behind the wheel of a bus or SUV. It could also mean guiding school kids around a National Park just a few miles from where you grew up. You might lead daylong tours, or you could be away for weeks at a time, sleeping in a tent at night. It all depends on what job you take!

As a guide, one of your most important jobs is to make the tour fun for your group. You must be able to teach the group about the things they see during the expedition. As an ecotour guide, you will make sure that your group does not

Life as an ecotour guide may mean putting on walking boots and a backpack or strapping on oxygen tanks and flippers.

WHAT QUALITIES ARE NEEDED TO BE A GOOD TOUR GUIDE?

- You must have a sense of fun and adventure.
- You must enjoy meeting new people and be able to get along with people of all ages.
- You must be a good group leader.
- You must be committed to caring for the environment.
- You must be practical and calm in an emergency. For example, if faced with a rockslide or avalanche, you will need to lead your group around or through the danger.
- You must be willing and able to carry out first aid.
- You must be physically tough! Rain could be pouring down and you might have an upset stomach, but you will still need to lead your group with a big smile on your face!

damage plants or frighten animals. You will also make sure that group members don't leave litter or carry out any activity that might damage the natural environment. Some tour guides train for the job by hooking up with experienced guides. Others start their career with a college or university course. This gives them the knowledge they will need to educate others in subjects such as botany (the plant world), biology, wildlife management, or the history and culture of a country.

No two days will ever be alike, and you will get the chance to meet a wide variety of people from all over the world!

Tour guides are often responsible for setting up and running an overnight camp for their group. Getting tents up, a fire lit, and a hot meal underway are all part of a long day's work!

Helping Wildlife with Tourist Dollars

For many people, seeing animals in their natural habitats is the ultimate dream holiday. Today, far too many animals are endangered because of hunting or the loss of their natural habitat to logging or the clearing of land for farms and villages. Ecotourism is helping protect these animals. Tourists see the animals in the wild, and funds from their trip are put toward conservation projects.

In Uganda, Africa, travelers can trek into the forests to watch families of mountain gorillas. There are fewer than 1,000 mountain gorillas left on Earth. When kept in captivity, these animals quickly die. The only place they will survive is in their natural mountain habitat. For many years, the mountain gorilla population was dropping. People were hunting gorillas for meat, and the gorillas were in competition for places to live with local people who cut down the forests to obtain firewood and to create farmland.

"I would like to see the tourism industry coming together to lobby African governments for greater protection and services for both the people and wildlife. Tourism provides the largest source of income for many southern and east African countries, and I believe that if the tourism industry leaders came together, we could help effect change."

Julia Nesbitt
Africa Program Director,
Wildland Adventures,
Seattle, Washington

Tourists in a safari jeep experience the thrill of getting close to a huge African elephant. There are laws that protect elephants from poachers who kill them for their ivory tusks, but elephants are still being killed. Conservation groups work with tourism companies to help local people earn money from wildlife tourism. This, in turn, gives local people a very good incentive to help protect animals such as elephants.

Conservation groups tried to protect the gorillas, but the animals were heading toward extinction.

Today, tourism has become an important way of protecting the gorillas for the future. People from around the world pay to see these animals. Local people are employed as guides and rangers to protect the animals and teach visitors about them.

Gorilla tourists trek through the forest with local guides. Funds from their trip are used to support conservation activities. Such activities might include paying the salaries of rangers who patrol the forest. These rangers keep the gorillas safe from poachers who might shoot them as bushmeat.

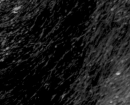

Money from gorilla trekking also goes to help conservation organizations with their work. It's not just the mountain gorillas that benefit from this work. When the forest is protected, many other species of mammals, birds, reptiles, and insects that live there will be protected, too.

The money that comes to Uganda from gorilla tourism is desperately needed by this poor country. Today, thanks to this new kind of tourism, the mountain gorilla is a leading source of export income!

CAREER PROFILE

HELPING WILDLIFE AND PEOPLE: AFRICA PROGRAM DIRECTOR

The Africa Program Director is responsible for travel arrangements to countries across Africa. I deal with customer sales, managing clients' bookings, communicating with our operators in Africa, and developing new programs and sales material. I'm also involved in overseeing the conservation and community development projects that are linked to our holidays. For example, we offer gorilla trekking safaris in Uganda. Our safaris support the work of the Dian Fossey Gorilla Fund International.

I arrive in the office around 7:00 A.M. so I can connect with my colleagues in Africa on the phone, despite the time difference. Much of my work is conducted over email. I respond to questions from existing clients and create custom adventures for new clients. I also read up on the latest news for the countries I work with. I travel once or twice a year to keep up-to-date on destination knowledge.

The thing I like best about my job is being an advocate for Africa. The Western world largely sees the worst of this remarkable continent, but I find that once people have the chance to visit and experience any place in Africa, they have to go back!

My advice to any person who wants to do my job is travel! Your best entry into the adventure ecotourism industry is firsthand destination knowledge.

Julia Nesbitt
Africa Program Director
Wildland Adventures
Seattle, Washington

Protecting the Planet and Travelers

As the popularity of ecotourism grows, people must work hard to prevent greenwashing from growing, as well. To ensure that eco-friendly travelers can trust the vacations they book or the hotels they stay in, certification programs are being set up. Some of these programs exist in individual countries, and others are international. Certification programs put in place sets of rules that detail how a company must work to protect the natural environment. These rules also spell out how tourist companies must protect the local people and the places where it arranges vacations. If a company is doing all the right things, it will become certified. Travelers who use that company will be able to see on the company's advertising materials or Web site that it has been checked and approved as abiding by all the principles of ecotourism.

A cruise ship in the Antarctic gives tourists the chance to see this incredible landscape and its wildlife. Cruise ships employ a wide variety of workers from crew members who sail the ship to chefs, bartenders, and cleaners.

Certification programs also provide possible career opportunities. People working in such programs are trained to know all the ways in which a company should be green. Once they are on the job, they visit and examine travel agencies, ecolodges, and other ecotourism businesses. They assess these businesses and report on whether they should be certified. Ecotourism assessors also visit businesses on an ongoing basis to make sure that as time passes and a business grows or changes, it has not lowered its standards.

ECOTEACH

Ecoteach is a U.S.-based organization that takes groups of teachers and students from middle school, high school, and college on trips to Costa Rica, Peru, and Mexico. The trips are part of an important exchange. North American students get to learn about the daily lives and culture of people in other parts of the world.

In exchange for this trip of a lifetime, the students help with conservation projects. Students might spend time planting trees to help rebuild a forest that has been destroyed by logging. They may work with scientists who are trying to save critically endangered sea turtles. The work can include tagging turtles so they can be tracked or transplanting turtle eggs from unprotected areas to protected areas of a beach. It may also include clearing trash from beaches to make it easier for the turtles to nest.

A sea turtle covers her eggs with sand on a nesting beach. When the baby turtles hatch from their eggs, they emerge from the sand and make a dash for the ocean.

TRAINING FOR YOUR ECOTOURISM CAREER

A gray whale rises from the ocean in front of a whale watching boat in San Ignacio Lagoon, Baja California, Mexico. If you feel marine biology could be a career for you, you might work on a whale watching boat or cruise ship telling tourists about the animals they see and giving educational lectures.

So, you have a passion for the environment, adventure, and travel. How do you get started and turn your interests into a career?

Start Studying

Ecotourism is the future of the travel industry. Many training schools, colleges, and universities have recognized this and now offer students courses in all aspects of ecotourism. Studying subjects such as biology and history may also be important if your work will include educating tourists about the natural world or historic places.

Get Online

You can also take an online course to gain both a solid background and professional certification in practicing ecotourism. The International Ecotourism Society offers a variety of courses that lead to a professional Certificate in Sustainable Tourism Management. The program includes courses on marketing a tourism destination, using the Internet to promote your business, and designing and setting up an ecolodge. It also provides courses in managing tourism to marine destinations or destinations with important links to history and other cultures.

There are even online courses you can take to become qualified to work as a tour guide. These courses will teach you how to identify fish, birds, animals, plants, and even types of rocks and landforms. They will also train you in how to set up a tour and how to lead your tour in a way that will be safe and enjoyable for your customers.

Volunteering—Giving and Receiving

Many young people first get involved in ecotourism as volunteers. Worldwide, there are many projects underway to help impoverished communities or natural habitats that are in danger. There is often a shortage of people working on these projects. In many cases, no salaries are offered, as every dollar is needed to carry out the core work. You might be asked to pay a fee to the project in order to take part, and you will need to pay for your own flights, accommodation, and food. You won't be earning a salary, but you will get the chance to travel to an exciting destination and learn new skills. In return, you will give back to the people and place.

Surf's Up!

Surfing is big business. As word gets out about the latest hot surfing destinations, tourism follows. Hotels spring up, and businesses with head offices thousands of miles from the waves move in. Often the local people have no opportunity to benefit from the surf dollars that are flooding into their area. Sometimes an area may be too poor to offer visitors any reason to stay. Surfers arrive, surf, and move on.

At the coastal town of Lobitos in Peru, it's a very different story. With world-class waves, Lobitos was a prime target for the surfing industry. A group of surfers decided that they would get there first, however. Their goal was to see if they could help the people of Lobitos benefit from the natural wonder on their doorsteps.

Pack a bag and get started on the adventure of a lifetime as a volunteer. You will get to see new places and learn new skills and languages.

TRAINING THAILAND'S ECO CHAMPIONS

When the 2004 Indian Ocean tsunami struck Thailand, it left many already disadvantaged people homeless and with little hope for the future. The Ecotourism Training Center (ETC), set up by American Reid Ridgeway, has offered a new start to a number of young Thai people. These students have been trained as undersea tour guides. They learned English and developed computer skills as part of their new career paths.

The young guides will play a key role in helping local people understand that tourism can be profitable for their country. They will also learn that this can happen only if the marine wildlife and coral reefs along their coastlines are still there. The guides will be on call to help with conservation efforts. In addition, ETC has started a business offering scuba diving and coastal ecotourism adventure tours.

A business named Sustainable Marine Adventures & Responsible Tourism (SMART) has also pitched in. SMART will employ the ETC graduates, and 10 percent of the company's income will go toward training more young people.

SURFING AND GIVING BACK: VOLUNTEER ON THE WAVES SURF PROGRAM

I'm from Long Island, New York. After earning a bachelor's degree in fine art photography, I now have my own photography business. Taking part in the WAVES surf program is the first time I've volunteered.

At Lobitos, I'm working with a local student, named Henry, to whom I am teaching photography. A typical day at WAVES might start with some surfing and then breakfast with other volunteers. After breakfast I prepare what I will be doing with Henry that day. At 1:30 P.M. we all go to lunch at a local family's home, and then there's some free time for surfing. In the late afternoon and early evening I work with Henry. Then all the volunteers prepare dinner and hang out.

The best thing about volunteering has been seeing the beautiful coast at Lobitos and meeting wonderful people—both locals and volunteers from around the world. My most memorable moments are seeing Henry get excited after capturing a great photo and pushing the younger kids into the waves at surf class.

I hope to continue working with WAVES in building a successful photography program. I will continue to work as a professional photographer and give back as much as possible.

Loreto Caceres
Volunteer for WAVES
Lobitos, Peru, South America

The surfers came up with a donation of 400 surfboards. They then got to work helping the local people learn to surf, swim, speak English, and take care of the natural environment. They also helped people start small businesses offering services to tourists such as surfboard repair.

With fewer than 50 percent of local kids graduating from high school, an important part of the program is working with children. Volunteers spend time teaching kids healthy activities such as surfing and swimming. They also give classes in English, healthy living, life skills for the future, and business skills. In addition to all of this, they teach the kids about conserving the environment.

Get researching online and find out if your interests are a good fit for a volunteer program to help people have a better life. The program might be in a country on the other side of the world or in the next town!

Now, as part of this surfing project, volunteers from around the world can come to Lobitos. Here, they can enjoy the surf and help the local people and children have a better future.

Get Started in Research

There are often volunteer positions available as scientific field researchers. Again, you will have to cover your costs. But you will be doing important conservation work and gaining valuable experience that could be useful if your dream is to work in wildlife tourism or as a tour guide.

The Earthwatch Institute is an organization that brings scientists and volunteers together to study and find solutions to the environmental problems threatening the world today. Each year, Earthwatch offers about 4,000 volunteers the chance to work in the field on scientific research programs. Volunteers might be working with the Aleut people of Alaska to help save seals. They might be tracking and monitoring jaguars, pumas, and spectacled brown bears in the Ecuadorian Andes. They might be studying how natural farming methods can turn vineyards in France into wildlife havens.

An Earthwatch volunteer helps capture a koala so that its malfunctioning radio collar can be replaced. She is helping with an Earthwatch study on the lives of koalas on St. Bees Island, Mackay, Queensland, Australia.

Start Your Ecotourism Career as an Intern

Another option to help you get your foot in the door is to look for work as an intern. An intern is a person, usually a young person, who works for a company in order to gain experience within that industry. Depending on where you are working, you may have to work for free or for a very small wage. Sometimes you will be offered financial help with travel costs.

An intern in an ecotourism travel agency or adventure tours company might work as an assistant to the sales or marketing team. You will probably answer the telephone and help with paperwork. As your knowledge grows, you may get a chance to help with arrangements for customers' vacations.

Left and opposite page: Whether you're making the coffee, filing, tidying up the office, or answering the telephone, your hard work and enthusiasm as an intern at a travel company will get your foot on the first rung of the ladder to your ecotourism career!

If you have a flair for writing and promotion, you might be given a marketing project to work on. For example, you might have to write material to raise people's awareness of the different tours the company offers on blogs and forums that discuss green travel options.

Whether you go to school to learn about ecotourism, put on your backpack and head off to get your hands dirty, or take a junior position where you can learn about the industry on a day-to-day basis, your career in ecotourism will be under way!

GREEN TOURISM CLOSER TO HOME

Maybe you could start an ecotourism business in your hometown! Could you offer a cycle or walking tour to visitors that would show them all those off-the-beaten-track places that only locals know? Perhaps a green business renting or repairing bicycles is for you.

Vacationing green doesn't have to mean weeks spent away from your home country in a tropical jungle. A green vacation can be a week spent at a beach just 50 miles (80 kilometers) from home. You could cycle to the beach. You could even stay in a tent that has no electricity, hot showers, or flushing toilets. This way, your accommodations produce no CO_2 emissions and do not use up gallons of water each day!

Staycations

Today, many people choose not to travel thousands of miles for a vacation. They make the decision to have what is popularly called a staycation. This means they vacation in their own country. Sometimes they stay in their own home and enjoy day trips to local places. This is a very environmentally friendly way to vacation, because you are not producing tons of CO_2 by flying or driving long distances.

Marc Bartschat combines his love of outdoor pursuits with running an ecotourism business.

It's also an option that makes good financial sense for many families when money is tight. Taking day trips during a staycation is a great way to support local conservation projects, wildlife centers, and parks.

Conservation Starts at Home

Local conservation projects and tourist attractions are also good places to look for an eco-friendly career in tourism closer to home. One career option is to become a park ranger. In national parks, rangers lead hikes and teach visitors about the plants and animals that can be found in the park. Parks need to be managed in a way that protects the natural habitat and ensures that any visitor disturbance is sustainable. This means that the presence of visitors should not damage the landscape for the future.

A park ranger talks to visitors during a guided tour of the Everglades National Park, Miami, Florida. Park rangers lead hikes, give talks on the local and natural history of the area, and answer a lot of questions. Park rangers enforce safety rules in the park and help if there is a medical emergency. They also chase off wildlife if a visitor is being bothered by one of the park's inhabitants!

CAREER PROFILE

WHEELIN' AROUND WASHINGTON: SEGWAY TOUR GUIDE AND OPERATIONS MANAGER

I began as a Segway tour guide while a student at George Washington University. Initially, I took the job to pay my rent and get some public-speaking experience. My first job was leading tours. I gradually moved up to running the everyday operations of the Washington, D.C., office. But leading tours is still my favorite part of the job. It's a blast!

When leading a tour, you start by teaching people how to ride the Segway PT ("personal transporter"). Then you take them around the city to see some of its national treasures. The best candidates for this kind of work are great with people, enjoy history, and have magnetic personalities and an eye for detail.

As cities get more crowded, large tour buses are putting more stress on cities' roads and transportation systems. Also, the last thing cities need is more smog. Developing "green" ways to see some of the world's best cities is a priority for this company. Although we aren't trying to change the world, we are certainly helping change the way tourists and locals sightsee!

John Voci
City Operations Manager
City Segway Tours of Washington, D.C.

Segway guide John Voci (center) is shown with a tour group on their Segways on the National Mall in Washington, D.C.

THE EDEN PROJECT

In Cornwall, in southwest England, the Eden Project is an eco-friendly tourist attraction. In 2009, it attracted over one million visitors. Housed under giant domes are gardens from many different habitats around the world. These habitats include an amazing rain forest. Here, visitors can see bananas growing, rubber trees, and a host of other full-size rainforest trees. Eden is like a zoo—for plants! It's a place where visitors can learn about Earth's plant life and its importance to our survival.

Tourists might only head to Eden for a day, but there is no doubt that it is all about ecotourism. Visitors can learn about cutting CO_2 emissions, recycling, growing food in a sustainable way for the future, protecting nature around the world—the list goes on! Eden doesn't just teach about these things. Teams from Eden have been involved in projects to replant forests and restore areas damaged by industries such as mining.

Eden understands that people need care, too. In the town of Podujevo, Kosovo (in the Balkan region of southeastern Europe), Eden was involved in creating a peace garden. The people of the town visit the garden to remember those who were killed there during a war in Kosovo in 1999.

Visitor attractions like Eden offer a variety of jobs. They range from scientists, to gardeners, to gift shop sales people, and restaurant chefs.

Visitors to the Eden Project get to walk through a real-life rain forest in England!

As one of the team of rangers, you will be working to make sure that goal is achieved.

Not everyone can afford to go on a safari to the grasslands of Africa or visit a rain forest in Brazil. Zoos and safari parks offer a close-to-home way for tourists to see wild animals and learn about the dangers the animals face in the wild. Today, most zoos are involved in conservation work. They might be breeding endangered animals to prevent them from becoming extinct. Some zoos are also funding research projects in wild

places with the money that the zoo earns from visitor entrance fees. These programs need people to staff and manage them.

If interacting with the public and animals is more to your liking, you might consider working as a zookeeper. A career as a zookeeper (also known as an animal keeper) will allow you to work hands-on with animals. You will also be involved in educating the tourists who visit and teaching people about the animals you care for. In some cases, zookeepers also perform research. As environmental awareness becomes a more pressing concern, keepers may also help develop the growing array of programs and exhibits that zoos offer today.

An animal keeper gives an educational talk to visitors while her two charges try to steal a snack!

Making Your Career Count

Today, travelers can use carbon offsetting when taking a flight. They can spend money on accommodations and tours that help support conservation projects and jobs for local people. They learn to take care not to

AGRITOURISM—A WORKING VACATION ON A FARM

Another vacation idea that has strong links to an eco-friendly lifestyle is agritourism. Many farms that grow food or raise animals in an organic way offer visitors the chance to stay and work on the farm. Visitors learn the skills to start their own farm or at least learn how to grow their own food in an eco-friendly, sustainable way. Sometimes tourists might stay on a farm and learn a skill such as cheese- or wine-making.

Farms often run volunteer programs, too. In return for learning farming skills and getting to spend a summer in a beautiful rural location, young people will work on the farm. Their duties may include fixing fences and farm buildings, planting and harvesting, or caring for animals.

harm the environment they are traveling through. With programs and goals like these, tourism can play a big part in fighting climate change, protecting wild places, and bringing different cultures together.

Your job in ecotourism could be part of all this. You might work in an office or in a mountain ecolodge, with tourists on the other side of the world, or with visitors to your hometown. Whichever path you take, you will know that you are helping to give like-minded people the trip of a lifetime, while protecting the planet for future generations.

It's a beautiful, big, wide world out there. Happy travels!

START YOUR GREEN FUTURE NOW...

It's exciting to have plans and dreams for the future. It's also exciting to try new things. Here are some fun projects to help you find out what you enjoy doing and to whet your appetite for your future career.

GET INVOLVED IN ECOTOURISM

Join The International Ecotourism Society's discussions on Facebook and Twitter. You will be able to find out all the latest information on ecotourism, learn about the coolest new places to visit, and share your own travel stories and ideas.

PRODUCE A GREEN PASSPORT FOR YOUR HOMETOWN

The United Nations Environment Programme has created "green passports" for some countries. These documents are downloadable. They help tourists plan their trips to countries such as Brazil, Costa Rica, and South Africa in the most sustainable way possible. Create a green passport for your hometown. What are the DOs and DONTs for visitors to your town? You might suggest that they use an out-of-town parking lot and ride the bus into town to cut down on pollution in the center of your town. You might recommend a café that serves food grown by local farmers instead of telling them to visit a large restaurant chain.

PLAN YOUR TOP TEN DREAM DESTINATIONS

Using guidebooks and the Internet, research places around the world that you would like to visit. Create a wish list of ten places you want to see. Is it possible to visit these places and still stick to the principles of ecotourism?

BE A GREEN TRAVEL WRITER

These days, plenty of tourism Web sites offer places where visitors can review restaurants, hotels, and visitor attractions. By posting your own comments online, you can try your hand at being a travel writer and never miss a chance to review a place you go to. If you visit a place that claims to be green or eco-friendly, make sure to report on whether the place lived up to its green credentials so other travelers can support it, too.

BECOME A TRAVEL AGENT

Plan a day trip for friends and family, and keep it green! Find the best way to travel to reduce CO_2 emissions. Research places to eat where you can obtain organic or locally produced food. Find fun things to do that are based on conservation and protecting the planet. To make sure everything runs like clockwork, plan an itinerary for your day.

BE SMART, BE SAFE!

Please get permission from the adult who cares for you before making trips to new places or volunteering in your free time. Always let him or her know where you are going and who you are meeting.

INDEX

ABOUT THE AUTHOR

Diane Dakers Diane has been a newspaper, magazine, television, and radio journalist since 1991. She is currently completing a master's degree in Journalism. Over the years, she has traveled by train, ferry, seabus, horse-drawn carriage, sailboat, subway, streetcar, tractor, and canoe. She does not own a car and relies on public transit, carpooling, and her own two feet to get where she needs to go.